The LeBaron Russell Briggs Prize
Honors Essays in English · 1970

MARLOWE'S "AGONISTS"

An Approach to the Ambiguity of His Plays

T0324428

MARLOWE'S "AGONISTS"

An Approach to the Ambiguity of His Plays

Christopher G. Fanta

Harvard University Press

Cambridge, Massachusetts

1970

Library of Congress Catalog Card Number 74-143220
SBN 674-55060-9

Printed in the United States of America

CONTENTS

MARLOWE'S "AGONISTS"

INTRODUCTION

English drama was at least six hundred years old and still in its infancy when Christopher Marlowe came to London in 1587. At the beginning of the wondrous fifty-year period during which popular drama quickly reached its majority and then its fullest bloom, he absorbed the whole tradition of the morality and hybrid-morality plays[1] and transformed it into what must be called—for its comparative psychological realism—a "modern" theater. As a poet he gave the English stage a dramatic poesy that for the first time combined true poetic quality with plausibility of characterization;[2] as a dramatist he demonstrated the unifying and spectacular value of a single, dominating superhero; and as a tragedian, together with Thomas Kyd, he forged the transition from the homiletic tragedies of the 1560's and 1570's to the great Shakespearean tragedies of the first decade of the seventeenth century.

Despite the recognized importance of his dramaturgic innovations, however, the moral content of Marlowe's plays[3] remains perplexingly ambiguous. In two particular areas of importance where one generally looks to find the direct imprint of a playwright's mind, Marlowe will not be cornered. He eludes us, first, when we turn to the utterances and actions of virtuous characters with whom the reader or viewer is invited to identify; such characters have no prominence in his plays. We search in vain to be guided to meaning by a Heavenly Man, Virtuous Life, or Just,[4] as in the homiletic tragedies, or by the John of Gaunts, Macduffs, Horatios, or Cordelias of Shakespeare.

Often, especially after *Tamburlaine the Great,* Part One, the dramatic conflicts of the plays involve two morally corrupt positions; the faulted or wholly evil protagonist collides not with the representative norm of the established world order but with "Machiavellian" policy, conquering ambition, or Mephistopheles himself. Marlowe leads us into the maelstrom of his tragic or farcical world with no apparent way leading out.[5] Nor can one a priori assume with Marlowe, as one might with Shakespeare, that a curse on both their houses implies a prescription for moderation. In direct contrast to Ulysses' famous speech in *Troilus and Cressida* on "degree, propriety, and place,"[6] Tamburlaine about fifteen years earlier abandoned moderation to the timid; and at least partially in the spirit of the exuberant young Marlowe, he proclaimed his credo:

> Nature, that framed us of four elements
> Warring within our breasts for regiment,
> Doth teach us all to have aspiring minds.
> > (*1 Tamburlaine,* II, vii, 18–20)

Marlowe eludes us again when we examine the out-
comes of his plays. How is one to interpret the deaths of
Tamburlaine, Barabas, and Faustus, the giant heroes of
the Marlovian canon? One reacts uncertainly, wavering
between regard for the justice of their downfalls and a
greater admiration for the grandeur of their ascents, while
at the same time—and here the confusion intrudes—one
at best only discontentedly accepts the order that outlives
them. In the homiletic tragedies, the comic-grotesque
treatment of the Worldly Man figure, ultimately carried
off to damnation by the Vice, patently establishes the
perspective of the moral lesson. Even in the possible
absence of any triumphant virtuous characters at the conclusion,[7] the righteous justification for the action is never
called into doubt. Similarly, the *de casibus* tradition of
tragedy represented an open moral text for princes and
kings, a *Mirror for Magistrates*[8] as it were, in which tyrants' lives were portrayed as clearly damnable and their
deaths as "deserved." On the other hand, in Shakespearean tragedy the lives of the tragic heroes derive meaning,
at least in part, from the reaffirmation of order that follows
their deaths. Out of the jarring clash between the tragic
protagonist and the destiny that shapes his end emerges
a reconstructed moral framework that is our debt to the
tragic strife. Marlowe's tragic vision, however, includes
neither unambiguous condemnation of the protagonist nor

the reintegration of the social structure after his fall: rather, it conjures a kind of limbo of moral claims and a vague sense of dissatisfaction with the fate of man.

Critical disagreement about Marlowe's message to his Renaissance audience reflects and thus helps to define the perceived ambiguity in the plays. Ever since Robert Greene charged Marlowe with "daring God out of heaven with that atheist Tamburlaine,"[9] one line of criticism has propounded the image of the heretical Marlowe whose heroes undermined the traditional Elizabethan morality with their atheistic, epicurean, or Machiavellian[10] heresies. In works such as *The Theatre of Gods Iudgements* and *The Thunderbolt of Gods Wrath against Hard-Hearted and stiffe-necked sinners,* sixteenth-century moralists interpreted Marlowe's death in a tavern brawl as God's retribution against a "Poet of scurrilitie" who gave "too large a swinge to his owne wit."[11] Nineteenth-century Romanticists such as Lamb and Swinburne cherished these very defiances in the name of the Promethean hero, perceiving in Marlowe and in his stage counterparts a lone, ever-striving spirit in quest of infinitude, challenging the forces of darkness and unreason for the benefit of common humankind.[12] Various contemporary critics, including Harry Levin, Una Ellis-Fermor, and Paul Kocher, have refined this Romantic icon to a more inclusive portrait in which the playwright, still a rebel, uses the framework of certain conventional theological and ethical assumptions, as in *Dr. Faustus*, only to challenge their doctrinal validity. In general, from this critical perspective Marlowe's own life, with its renegade and dissolute aspects highlighted, appears in the mirror from which nature is recorded in the aspirations and blasphemies of his overreaching heroes; and he is considered "one of the most highly subjective writers of his age."[13]

A second group of twentieth-century scholars, who have been dubbed "neo-orthodox moralists,"[14] have challenged the notion of Marlowe's radicalism. As if displaying the tarnished underside of a shiny coin, such critics as Roy Battenhouse, Douglas Cole, and Alfred Harbage point to the sins of the aspiring heroes—to their greed or ambition or lust for forbidden knowledge—and to their just punishment by death as evidence of traditional values upheld. By this view the overreacher's transgression of those standards which Elizabethan audiences are said to have held sacrosanct becomes vice rather than virtue, his death constitutes just retribution more than tragic doom, and defiance gives place to orthodoxy. In fact, all plays publicly performed after 1581 underwent censorship by the Master of the Revels, a deputy of the Queen, and therefore no heterodox material treating the topics of contemporary English church and state could have been presented undisguised.[15] In dealing with the facts of Marlowe's life, critics in this camp tend to emphasize his six years of theological training at Corpus Christi College, Cambridge; and they regard his portrayal of aspiring heroes, whose aspirations, they note, vary from Faustus' pursuit of "knowledge infinite" to the Guise's murderous political ambitions in *The Massacre at Paris,* as nonsubjective dramatic creativity.

One critical study of particular importance, David Bevington's *From "Mankind" to Marlowe,* approaches the consistent ambiguity of the plays by a study of Marlowe's use of the structural mechanisms inherited from the popular drama. "It is the interplay between moral structure and secular content," Bevington writes, that defines "the fascination and yet the ambiguity of the dramatic message."[16] According to his thesis, while Marlowe imbued his heroes, drawn mostly from secular sources, with a *grandeur d'âme* and consequent appeal irrespective of any homiletic context, he also employed a traditional structure that by its linearity[17] and implications of cause and effect of necessity imposes an ill-fitting moral lesson. The argument is compelling: it seems to balance the fervor that inspirits Marlowe's protagonists with the claims for the moral rightness of their downfalls; and it offers an explanation for our uneasiness, especially in the later plays, about the conditions under which "justice" is implemented. However, ambiguity in the creation may also result from

6

ambivalence in the creator, and one must inquire whether rather than acting as a structural "trap," the forms of the plays give expression to a duality of outlook, and equally to a gradually developed pessimism, that characterized Marlowe's mind. This discussion, then, will look beyond the formal aspects of the plays to the motivating intellect that, like any other artistic imagination, adapted forms (within the practical limits of Elizabethan stagecraft) to the primary purpose of communicating thoughts and feelings.

With few exceptions Marlowe's minor characters are monotone stick-figures, sometimes more like stage props than like people; yet the key to exploring the less fiery side of his mind and, thereby, to understanding something of the dual thrust of his thought lies with a particular set of these minor characters: the handful of weak but virtuous persons who command his respect. Repeatedly Marlowe makes weakness, often combined with gullibility, cowardice, stupidity, or cunningless hypocrisy, the object of his caustic irony: the effete and craven Mycetes, king of Persia, and the two faithless friars, Jacomo and Barnardine, for instance, are first impaled by Marlowe's wit and then expeditiously done away with by Tamburlaine and Barabas, respectively. However, although they have no power or guile, Zenocrate and Olympia in *Tamburlaine,*

Abigail in *The Jew of Malta,* Prince Edward in *Edward II,* and the Old Man in *Dr. Faustus* are portrayed with a dignity which convinces us of Marlowe's attraction to them. Two women, a young girl, a boy, and an old man— these are the exponents of Marlowe's gentler spirituality, the calm lake in the stormy tumult of his vision.

Through these characters Marlowe's "other" voice receives utterance, one not crying out to "topless hills" and "quenchless fires"[18] but filled with the less hyperbolic sentiments of pity, mercy, mutability, faith in Christian grace, and a longing for peace without struggle. Above all else, these five characters show "simplicity," that which in Marlowe's vocabulary most Christians profess but do not practice, the exact opposite of Machiavellian policy. In following their fortunes, one observes that Marlowe's regard for their innocence does not in general derive from any subtle strength or worldly effectiveness which virtue confers on them; Marlowe's world is too tough, too unsentimental, to allow right without might much courtesy. In this respect the sex or, in the case of the men, the age of the five personae is telling: most if not all of their roles would have been filled by boy actors[19] playing along side men of such stature as the celebrated Edward Alleyn. Rather, then, virtue for itself, or as a kind of personal haven, evokes a responsive if low-keyed note from Marlowe, a note which sounds from another side of the poet than from the brash, man-of-the-world Marlowe who is said to have preached irreligion wherever he went.[20]

This more muted voice is heard in numerous places throughout Marlowe's works, sometimes even given expression by the overreachers themselves; but in each play it becomes focused into at least one minor role, so that one can explore how Marlowe perceived the function of "simplicity" in this world by considering the way in which he develops these parts. They bear significance not for any depth of personality—of which, admittedly, one finds little enough—but for their function in the plot, for their words and actions of exceptional (by Marlowe's standards) virtue, and most important, for their relation to the heroes and the light they shed on the heroic endeavor. They qualify our vision of the overreacher and suggest something of Marlowe's own ambivalent attitude, for more and more radically in the sequence of the plays they challenge the means and the ends of the heroes' gigantic graspings, setting against all the bombast, the glorious adventure, and the laurels of the quest a peacefulness of self and an awareness of the ravages of that quest. They are "agonists" in Marlowe's gallery of giant protagonists, innocent sufferers "Doomed for a certain term to walk the night" of this earth's ruthlessness.

Within each play the effect of the contrast between the overreacher and the countercurrent minor figure may indicate a more or less deliberate effort by Marlowe to temper our conception of his protagonist, creating ambiguity as the expression of his own reservations or, perhaps, fears about the effort to exceed one's own humanity. In the spaces between the plays, however, one can discern a development that, like virtually all significant trends in any series of noncyclic works, reveals a nonconscious evolvement of the artist's sensibility. At first, in the Scythian Eden of his imagination, Marlowe perceives no irresoluble conflict between aspirations "All air and fire"[21] and sentiments more of "the massy earth" (1 Tamburlaine, II, vii, 31) like pity and the notion of fragile mortality: the two impulses could be combined within one man or adduced to him by marriage; and the world would stoop to the triumphant union. With time, however, the optimism of the first part of *Tamburlaine* passes to despair at the hellfires of *Dr. Faustus,* and the schism between the overreacher and the agonist develops and then widens to open hostility.

Tamburlaine the Great

With only slight exaggeration one might say that Marlowe's career as a popular dramatist began with that typifying moment when the six-and-a-half feet tall Edward Alleyn as Tamburlaine disdainfully threw off his shepherd's weeds, the symbol of his low birth, and exposed beneath them a suit of armor as "more beseeming Tamburlaine" (I, ii, 43). Alleyn's physical presence as he raged and stalked so that "his poore hearers hayre quite vpright sets"[22] was itself a metaphor for the towering aspirations of all the overreachers fermenting in Marlowe's imagination:

> Of stature tall, and straightly fashionèd,
> Like his desire, lift upwards and divine.
> (II, i, 7–8)

One can hardly appreciate the startling impression that the early performances of *1 Tamburlaine* must have created: the blank verse is adapted more successfully than ever before to the syntactical patterns of dramatic speech,[23] including those "high astounding terms" promised in the Prologue (l. 5); a panoply of color and spectacle fills the stage like a series of ornate tableaux;[24] and most of all,

Tamburlaine treads the "wheel of Fortune" from its base as a peasant to its height as world conqueror, and then he arrests its motion. The cycle is completed not with death but with his order to "Cast off your armor, put on scarlet robes" (V, ii, 461), and with preparation for his marriage to Zenocrate.

Virtually all available evidence indicates that the first part of *Tamburlaine* was conceived, as without question it was performed,[25] independently of Part Two, in which Tamburlaine finally meets his death.[26] Although the Prologue invites one to view Tamburlaine's "picture in this tragic glass" (l. 6), tragedy, in Sidney's sense of that which "maketh kinges feare to be Tyrants" and "teacheth the vncertainty of this world,"[27] befalls only Tamburlaine's enemies in Part One. In fact, the triumphant conclusion of the play classifies it in the same category with *The Famous Victories of Henry the Fifth* (1586) and *The Comical History of Alphonsus, King of Aragon* (1591),[28] both likewise celebrations of victorious conqueror-kings who in the end confirm the peace by marrying the princess-daughters of their opponents. However, as the Scythian shepherd differs in rank from young Hal in the Eastcheap tavern and from Alphonsus disguised and in exile, so Marlowe's play differs in spirit from the other two; for Hal and Alphonsus are rightful heirs to crowns while Tamburlaine is destined, as one of George Peele's characters laments, "To chástise and to menace lawful kings."[29] Marlowe's conception of human potentialities first takes form, then, as a vision of the limitless capacity of manly *virtù*, independent of royal blood, to subdue circumstance to its will while boastfully defying the fickleness of heaven, the hierarchies of earth, and the punishment of hell.

In one sense the entire play is designed to illustrate Tamburlaine's proud assertion

> That virtue solely is the sum of glory,
> And fashions men with true nobility.
>
> (V, ii, 126–127)

With remarkable dexterity Marlowe fashions Tamburlaine's "true nobility" solely out of his hero's Herculean powers and the magic of his own "mighty line." As his opponents grow in an incremental crescendo of merit and power, so Tamburlaine's heroic stature builds on their sequential defeats. At the same time, by the self-characterization of his "working words" (II, iii, 25)—his hyperbolic threats and promises and general presentiments —we are urged toward the conception of a virtual demigod who, as he says, makes "the Fatal Sisters sweat" (V, ii, 391). When Zenocrate accepts Tamburlaine as her husband and he in turn crowns her his queen of Persia, there can remain no doubt as to his achievement of nobility.

Zenocrate represents more than the dessert to a "course of crowns" (stage direction, IV, iv, 105) just as Tamburlaine's claim to nobility goes deeper than his military conquests: as he, besides being a warrior-tyrant, is a poet, lover, and aesthete, so she is an embodiment and object of expression of the milder strains of his character. She poses against Tamburlaine's regimen of murderous wars the countervalues of love and pity, but for the most part his personality subsumes both ethics. At this point Marlowe envisions no schism between the conqueror and the lover in a man: Tamburlaine openly confesses to a startled Theridamas his love for Zenocrate, while Zenocrate willingly participates in the verbal combat with the Turkish queen, Zabina, that is the metaphoric counterpart of Tamburlaine's battle with the Turkish king, Bajazeth.

When Marlowe has Tamburlaine attack Damascus in the land where Zenocrate was born and where her father rules as Soldan of Egypt, he boldly tests the limits within which love and relentless ambition can remain bound fast. Zenocrate's tearful pleas for her countrymen and the explicit innocence of the Damascene virgins run a tilt against Tamburlaine's "peremptory customs" of war, the finality of the black flags that symbolize total destruction; and the outcome leaves the virgins hanged from the city walls. Having ordered the rest of the victims put to the sword, Tamburlaine deliberates on the power which beauty works in his soul when Zenocrate entreats for her father's life. He concludes that beauty does not threaten martial discipline with effeminacy; rather,

> any warrior that is rapt with love
> Of fame, of valor, and of victory,
> Must needs have beauty beat on his conceits.
>   (V, ii, 117–119)

Tamburlaine sees himself as "thus conceiving and subduing both" (l. 120)—a poet and conqueror of both beauty and the discipline of war: immediately after the soliloquy he orders the encaged Bajazeth brought forth and demands from a soldier prompt news of Damascus' ransacking, but later he spares the Soldan's life.

Tamburlaine's self-image is not accurate, however; and his cruelties, particularly to the guiltless virgins and to Bajazeth and Zabina, threaten the tenuous union of simplicity and warmaking. Zenocrate's lament upon seeing Bajazeth's and Zabina's battered bodies, their brains struck out in suicide against the iron bars of the cage, sums up all of the pity and sense of worldly mutability which Tamburlaine can neither conceive nor subdue. She looks upon sights which would have made, as she says, "the angry god of arms / To break his sword and mildly treat of love" (V, ii, 263–264) and begs forgiveness for not having sooner pitied the Turks' mistreatment. Tamburlaine's reaction to the same scene makes an explicit contrast with Zenocrate's gentle humanity: he perceives "All sights of power to grace my victory" (V, ii, 411). As the emissary of our common morality, Zenocrate demonstrates where the monstrous replaces the heroic in Tamburlaine's all-consuming ascent toward nobility; where we feel repulsed at his needless savagery, she repents his inhumanity and gives warning, as will Abigail and the Old Man after her, to "Those that are proud of fickle empery" (V, ii, 289).

Although Tamburlaine refuses to be, as the Governor of Damascus would have him, "a loving conqueror" (V, i, 23), Zenocrate ultimately receives him as "my conquering love" (V, ii, 379). Having revealed the chasm which separates the overreaching hero from spiritual purity, Marlowe seals it up again with Tamburlaine's show of mercy to the Soldan and his marriage to Zenocrate. Like Zenocrate we are meant to accept the whole image of the superman, with his Herculean strengths and his Herculean cruelties.[30] Marlowe as yet admits no split between the aspiration and the achievement; and in the end, as Tamburlaine wins both the queen of beauty and the crown of war, one is left with a sense of wonderment at this celebration of mortal man's indomitability. Later in Marlowe's career, the aspiration comes to foretell the fall and the agonists more and more directly oppose the courses of the heroes. As a result, the moral schemata of the plays become more obscure, optimism turns toward pessimism, and the dual visions, the aspiring and the countercurrent visions, grow irreconcilable.

As various critics have noted,[31] after the popular success[32] of his first work for the public theater, Marlowe constructed the second part of *Tamburlaine* along many of the same lines as Part One, but he infused it with a considerably different tone. The form of the play again employs an episodic series of conquests to heighten Tamburlaine's posture as an "earthly god" (I, vi, 11), yet into this framework there intrudes the reality of death and, more, the recalcitrance of human affairs to bend to a single will. Much of the play reiterates Tamburlaine's heroic and appealing attributes; yet again and again while Tamburlaine continues victorious in battle, one becomes aware that people and events are eluding his control, until finally the breath of life itself reveals its independence. In a play where one of Tamburlaine's soldiers, Almeda, betrays him and where his enemy, Callapine, escapes his grasp, where the beautiful Olympia and Calyphas, Tamburlaine's son, are killed, and where Zenocrate and Tamburlaine themselves die, one senses Marlowe's embryonic tragic vision emerging from behind an essentially "comic" structure like that of Part One.[33]

The transitional position of the play in the Marlovian

canon is suggested by the way in which Zenocrate's role looks both backward to Part One and forward to *The Jew of Malta*. Her first words entreat an end to the wars, "Sweet Tamburlaine, when wilt thou leave these arms" (I, iv, 9), and in her waning health she observes the operation of "enforced and necessary change" (II, iv, 46) as it transmutes all things mortal into dust. As in Part One, she plays the gentle and contemplative humanist, both the opposite and the extension of the militaristic man of action, who draws his own blood to demonstrate his fearlessness and lectures his sons on strategic fortifications. In her farewell to her sons, she reaffirms her sanction of Tamburlaine's quest at the same time that she draws attention to the different meaning of her own life: "In death resemble me, / And in your lives your father's excellency" (II, iv, 75–76).

Zenocrate too must die, and in this development from Part One her role begins to prefigure the conflicts that will draw each of the subsequent agonists further apart from his corresponding protagonist. No disaffection springs between Tamburlaine and Zenocrate, yet her death occurring relatively early in the play acts like the cleavage of a vital appendage from Tamburlaine's psyche: as though a counterbalancing weight had suddenly been loosed, after Zenocrate's death Tamburlaine's fury rages more desperately, his threats against man and the gods grow increasingly more strident.[34] In the madness of his grief Tamburlaine would make war against heaven and hell; "Raving, impatient, desperate, and mad" (II, iv, 112), he has Zenocrate's body preserved in a sheet of gold to be kept in his train, and he has the town of her death—inhabitants and all—annihilated. The symbolic value of his tyrannies, for instance his making the Turkish emperor serve as his footstool in Part One, shades into an awesome gesture of futility and inane violence as the object of his terror, ultimately Fate itself, proves more and more unyielding to attack by force.

Although Zenocrate's emblematic presence is early removed from the action, her values of fidelity and peacemaking reappear, fragmented, in the person of Olympia, the captive widow of an opposing captain; to a lesser and more uncertain extent in Tamburlaine's half-cowardly, half-pacifistic son, Calyphas; and in some lines of Theridamas pleading before Tamburlaine for Calyphas' life. Olympia's role is the least important of the five agonists, but it represents an explicit example of the type: innocent and even heroic, she maintains her love for her dead husband and son in the face of promises of wealth and offers of new affection; and to protect her honor she contrives her own death. Like Zenocrate in Part One, she is "the queen of chastity" (IV, iii, 96); and like Zenocrate in Part Two, she "dies well," rejecting Theridamas' love the better to "meditate on death, / A fitter subject for a pensive soul" (IV, iii, 26–27).

To some extent the scene of Olympia's death is part of a tradition—from *Horestes* (1567) to *Macbeth*—of episodes, related only tangentially to the main plot, which portray the ravages that war wreaks on the guiltless common people.[35] More important for this discussion, she also further exemplifies Tamburlaine's failing ability to master nature—human and physical—to continue to turn all that he touches to success. Although Tamburlaine himself never confronts Olympia, we have come to associate Theridamas, his arch-lieutenant, with him; and when Theridamas woos the Zenocrate-like Olympia and mourns her death in the style of Tamburlaine, we cannot avoid the intimation that she has eluded Tamburlaine's grasp as much as Theridamas'.[36]

Without examining the character of Calyphas in any detail (for he obviously is not a spiritually pure and wholly admirable figure, as are the five agonists considered), one might note that his cowardice cum Falstaffian "discretion" is like a poisoned limb which Tamburlaine excises by stabbing Calyphas to death. As with the virgins of Damascus, the "argument of arms" (IV, ii, 25) must overrule natural sympathy, expressed here by Theridamas and Calyphas' brothers; but like the gash that Tamburlaine earlier incised in his own arm, this wound, too, is inflicted by his own hand and against his own body. The fact that Marlowe invented the character of Tamburlaine's cowardly son[37] and gave him lines that, no matter how much one tries to shed modern predispositions, seem to resonate with ironic jabs at the way of wars further suggests that in 2 *Tamburlaine* Marlowe begins to call into question the value of the overreaching vision, just as his virtuous minor characters will come to challenge it in the later plays.

With the absence of a figure like Zenocrate to guide our moral perspective at the end of the play, the path for ambiguity is laid wide. The moral significance of Tamburlaine's death following closely upon his burning of the Koran and other "superstitious books" (V, i, 172) hides behind an impenetrable maze of possible interpretations. Depending upon whether one considers the connection between Tamburlaine's blasphemies and his disease causal or coincidental and whether Mohammed or, behind the guise of euphemism, Christ is taken as the object of his attacks, the episode becomes variously orthodox or heterodox and Tamburlaine's oversized aspirations appear damned or simply ended.

Although the Prologue offers the view that in Tamburlaine's death "murderous Fates throw all his triumphs down" (l. 5), one may overemphasize the extent to which the play takes on the character of a "tragical discourse" as a result of the hero's fall. Marlowe does not draw a retributive or homiletic meaning from Tamburlaine's death. Unlike Thomas Preston in the "Lamentable Tragedie" of *The Life of Cambises, King of Percia* (1561), he characteristically refrains from the gratuitous moralism of the hero's self-recrimination—"A iust reward for my misdeeds my death doth plaine declare" (l. 1172). Furthermore, since anyone who was acquainted with the history of Tamburlaine would have known of the disintegration of his empire after his death,[38] the virtual exclusion from the ending of any intimation of this fact, with its readily extractable moral implications, suggests that Marlowe by no means meant to transform his superhuman hero into an object lesson for tyrants.

Rather, just as Faustus must learn from Mephistopheles the reality of the existence of hell, so Tamburlaine at last faces the inescapable truth of his mortality: "Tamburlaine, the scourge of God, must die" (V, iii, 248). The difference between Faustus' fearful damnation and Tamburlaine's peaceful death or, again, the distance between Tamburlaine's relatively complacent acceptance of his death and Barabas', Edward's, and Faustus' struggles against their violent demises is a measure of Marlowe's deepening despair for the fulfillment of the overreaching vision. In *2 Tamburlaine* the note of failed optimism first sounds.

In R[obert] W[ilson]'s *The Three Ladies of London*
(1581) a Turkish judge grieves at the wicked state of human affairs where "Iewes seeke to excell in Christianitie,
and Christians in Iewisnes."[39] The moral framework, as
one would expect in an interlude, is everywhere explicit:
in a world in which virtually everyone, including Love and
Conscience, is drawn in pursuit of Lucar, a Jew who for-
goes his ducats lest a Christian merchant forswear his God
appears to be a Jewish saint among Christian thieves.
Similarly, "the wind that bloweth all the world" in *The
Jew of Malta* is seen to be "Desire of gold" (III, v, 3, 4,),
but Marlowe exempts neither Turks nor Christians nor
Jews from the sin of avarice. The Turks use policy to ex-
tort money from the Maltese; the Christian governor of
Malta, Ferneze, issues a sham decree to rob Barabas, the
Jew; two friars attempt to blackmail Barabas with in-
formation received in confession; and the thugs Ithamore,
Bellamira, and Pilia-Borza do blackmail him with their
knowledge of his crimes.

The moral confusion of the play more closely resembles
a work like the anonymous *Farce of the Worthy Master
Pierre Patelin* (ca. 1469),[40] where, in the absence of any
apparent moral code, five "cozeners" play at outwitting
one another and capping each other's clever devices. How-

ever, the analogy again falls short, for Marlowe's characters do not "play" at the use of policy: their antagonisms are vicious and the stakes of their contests are life and death. The combination of farcical structure and Marlowe's bitterest salvos of irony against greed, religious intolerance, and Machiavellian policy engendered a play precisely if tersely characterized by T. S. Eliot as a farce of "savage comic humour."[41] Description of *The Jew of Malta* as "farce" is not meant here as a historical categorization—for Elizabethans probably would have received the play as a revenge tragedy[42]—but as an insight into the nature of its moral ambiguity.

With Barabas' famous speech to Ithamore enumerating his former villainies, beginning, "As for myself, I walk abroad a' nights / And kill sick people groaning under walls" (II, iii, 171–172), a shift in tone takes place. Barabas' pursuit of revenge slips into villainy, his *virtù* of survival in a hostile society for the most part is transformed into evil deeds, and Machiavellian policy runs wild except when challenged by more policy. The order and supposed justice of the state fade into the background, and Barabas is allowed to do his worst. Marlowe is demonstrating, I believe, exactly what is the "worst" that unchecked policy can do. One of the first questions that he poses probes the role, if any, of virtuous simplicity in such a world, as Abigail comes to perceive it to be, of loveless, pitiless, and impious savages.

Marlowe approaches this question by a technique of "double-exposure":[43] upon the first frame of Abigail's mock entrance into the "new-made nunnery" (I, ii, 310), he superimposes a second frame of her serious readmission after the death of Don Mathias, her lover. In the former scene, by clever stage-timing and the use of irony, Marlowe manages to show Abigail's conversion, which to orthodox Christian audiences probably implied the salvation of her soul,[44] to be entirely undesirable for both her life and soul. We know her to be perfectly virtuous, characterized, as *The Overreacher* points out, by the first four words she speaks: "Not for my self . . ." (I, ii, 229);[45] and we can laugh at the strange order of things whereby she must "seem to them as if [her] sins were great" (I, ii, 287) in order to be admitted.

By the time of the second frame of this double-exposure, however, the kind of world in which Abigail lives has altered to one where vengeance gluts itself at will. Christians wrong Jews, and Jews revenge beyond the bounds of the *lex talionis.* Her lover having been murdered by her father's schemes, Abigail turns now in sincerity to the church as sanctuary from a vicious world. There is a saddened wisdom in her words to the friar:

And I was chained to follies of the world,
But now experience, purchasèd with grief,
Has made me see the difference of things.
(III, iii, 60–62)

Like Olympia and the early Zenocrate, she preserves her
chastity, symbol of maidenly honor, and dies in exemplary
fashion. Because of her language and attitudes (for example, "And witness that I die a Christian" [III, vi, 39]),
we come to associate her virtue with her Christian faith;
and in this dramatic context we tend to approve of her
conversion and escape from evil. It would appear that in
"true" Christian faith, virtuous simplicity finds strength
and encouragement and ultimately salvation.

Marlowe has more to say about Christianity, however.
Following Abigail's death, he begins his parody of the
lecherous, covetous friars, Jacomo and Barnardine; and
one is given in effect a third exposure of this conversion
theme in Barabas' pretended intention to become a Christian and give away all of his money to one of the friars'
houses. His entreaty to be allowed to convert is a hilarious
mixture of parodied prejudices against Jews, flaunted pride
in his wealth, and mockery of the severity of Christian
penance. Under the satiric tone, however, there lies the
serious suggestion that the church, corrupted as an in-
stitution by unholy friars such as these, offers nothing
desirable or even relevant to one of the energy and mental

power of Barabas. In relation to someone not seeking to escape from the world but wholeheartedly causing its turmoil, the church fails as a force for social order and a restrainer of worldly evil.

Not only does the play demonstrate Marlowe's ambivalent attitude toward Christian faith, of which more will be said in connection with *Dr. Faustus,* but it reveals the split, now irreparable, that separates the protagonist from the agonist. At first Abigail helps her father to recover the money extorted by the false Christians, but when he pursues "revenge" against the guilty and innocent alike, she turns from him. These representatives of the two strains of Marlowe's thought can never again be harmonized once Barabas, having murdered Abigail, mentions casually to Pilia-Borza: "You know I have no child" (IV, v, 44).

Abigail's voice is silenced by her father's treachery, and Barabas is killed by Ferneze's treachery. It has been noted that one can feel no pity for Barabas at his death;[46] rather, one has a sense of relief at the silencing of this agent of undirected, universal hatred, who even with his last breath cries out against the "Damned Christians, dogs, and Turkish infidels!" (V, v, 86). But one feels, too, a profound uneasiness at the success of Ferneze's "capping" trick, which plunges Barabas into the cauldron. Malta fails resoundingly to cope with Barabas—in a sense, it fails to cope with the product of its own weaknesses—

and instead turns to the use of treachery to extinguish treachery.

Unable to bring justice to bear against Barabas, Ferneze practices the tactics of Machiavellian policy and shows, as it were, "A Jew's courtesy." After all the machinations of policy and twists of fate, the same corrupt, hypocritical governor remains securely in command of Malta, now with all its apparent enemies subdued. With Marlowe, as with most satirists, one of the greatest villains is the status quo, yet Marlowe gives the victory to the representative of the established order. Not even Ferneze's maddening self-righteous tone has been pierced; behind the ironically peaceful concluding lines lies the gloom of frustrated change.

Along with Marlowe's dream of the ability of a man to overreach the limitations of his society and to become, if only temporarily, more than a man, there resides in his maturer works an equally characteristic lack of faith that that overreacher can meaningfully bring change and new life to his society. And the hope embodied in Abigail's innocence was snuffed out before the beginning of Act IV.

The Troublesome raigne and lamentable death of Edward the Second, King of England

At the conclusion of *Edward II,* the newly-crowned King Edward III brings down vengeance on Mortimer and

Isabella, the instigators of his father's murder; and he offers his tears before the hearse of the dead king as "witness of my grief and innocency" (V, vi, 102). Throughout the strange unraveling of circumstance that first takes Prince Edward to France with Queen Isabella as the King's envoy and then brings him back to Engand as the nominal head of an army at war with his father, the young Edward remains free from the political intrigues and personal antipathies that taint all of the other players in the drama of state, except perhaps the Earl of Kent. The peace that Edward III establishes by Mortimer's overthrow, with its promise for an end to civil strife, marks one of the rare moments in Marlowe's plays where "innocency" triumphs over the policy of a "Machiavel." It is a fragile victory, however, demonstrative more of Marlowe's effort to believe than of the firm conviction of his faith: belief in the possibility that out of the tragic conflict may emerge a more lasting social order and a finer morality hesitatingly asserts itself only to be qualified by the diminutive characterization of Edward III. "The king is yet a child" (V, vi, 17), to Mortimer "a paltry boy" (V, vi, 57), and his strength is but the power of his tears to move the council of peers.

The last scenes of the play ring more loudly with Edward II's agonized death cry, "a waileful noyse" which in 1327 "did move many within the castell and towne of Berkley to compassion,"[47] than with his son's demands for a just revenge. Edward's passivity at his murderers' hands contrasts with Richard II's active struggle against his assassins in Shakespeare's play about Edward's historical mirror-image, and it epitomizes the frustrating weakness that plagues most of King Edward's reign. Especially when seen against the irrepressible assertion of will in *Tamburlaine,* the bold gesture is everywhere muted in *Edward II:* overreaching desires are frustrated, actions are negated by counteractions. Nor can Prince Edward escape being swept along by the momentum of that "strange exchange" (V, i, 35) "Where lords keep courts, and kings are lock'd in prison!" (V, iii, 64): he would oppose only the King's flattering advisors, but he in fact leads an army that dethrones his father; he would once more see his imprisoned father, who had likewise pleaded for a last visit with Gaveston, but his request is refused; he would spare the life of his uncle, the Earl of Kent, but he cannot. Justice comes finally as an eddy thrown up against the current of frustrations dominating the action; it is a victory without conviction in the worldly power of "simplicity."

Whereas much of the ambiguity in *The Jew of Malta* results from the absence of a moral framework, in the early acts of *Edward II* uncertainty attends the profusion of ethical and political claims bandied between the King and his nobles. Edward maintains his passionate affection for the "base-born" Gascon, Piers Gaveston, and his compulsive liberality toward all his minions "Despite of times, despite of enemies" (III, ii, 147), but first the barons and then his brother Kent and wife Isabella protest Gaveston's unworthiness and the ruinous condition of the commonwealth. Edward defends his right of absolute rule; his enemies rebel avowedly "for the good of the country." At the heart of the presentation of the political controversy lies the Elizabethan ambiguity about rebellion: though universally condemned in theory, revolt against evil kings at times seemed a necessity of practical politics.[48] And in the midst of the tragedy of state Marlowe probes the irony motivating King Edward's personal tragedy: the King drives from him all those who "naturally would love and honor [him]" (I, i, 100) for the sake of a man whom he cherishes "Because he loves me more than all the world" (I, iv, 77).

F. P. Wilson has described the Earl of Kent as "a point of reference," "the one character in the play upon whom the affections can rest, the one character—apart from the young Prince Edward—whose concern for the King is wholly untouched by jealousy, hatred, lust, or self-aggrandizement."[49] Indeed, Kent comes closer than any other character in Marlowe's plays to serving as a guide to moral judgment, but his desertion of the King's court and subsequent repentance of his "unnatural revolt" (IV, v, 18) undermine his moral authority. Like the common people, said to favor now the King, now the rebelling Mortimer, and now again the deposed King, Kent reflects the coarse movements of popular sentiment more than he directs our sympathies. He is not, like Shakespeare's John of Gaunt, "a prophet new inspired,"[50] nor like Prince Edward wholly blameless; but possibly he indicates the direction of greater clarity in which a maturer Marlowe might have developed, had temporal maturity been Marlowe's fate.

For a brief while after his initial victory over the nobles, King Edward enjoys a surge of new-felt power; with a rebirth of confidence he proclaims, "Edward this day has crowned him king anew" (III, iii, 77). Not long thereafter, however, he is found cowering in disguise at the Abbey of Neath, resting his head on the Abbot's lap as if thereby to shut out all his cares. Resistance becomes useless; suffering is his only part:

> The wren may strive against the lion's strength,
> But all in vain: so vainly do I strive.
>
> (V, iii, 34–35)

In this context Prince Edward's role performs two functions: it gives form to the play by rounding the action into a completed whole; and it attempts to formulate a meaningful vision of life, or here specifically of kingship, created out of the meaninglessness of suffering and death. Neither in earlier chronicle-history plays[51] nor in Holinshed's *Chronicles* would Marlowe have found precedents for this development of character and plot.

The chronicle histories prior to *Edward II*, including Shakespeare's three *Henry VI* plays, were organized chiefly as surveys of a given period, typically running several parallel strands of action without giving particular stress to any one dramatic conflict.[52] In *3 Henry VI*, for example, the life and death of the foolish King Henry becomes submerged beneath the wealth of detail concerning "Who loses and who wins, who's in, who's out" between the houses of York and Lancaster, and at the end Gloucester's plottings foretell continued turmoil. Marlowe, on the other hand, omits or condenses a great deal of historical material, highlights the interrelated rising or falling fortunes of Edward II, Mortimer, and the Prince,[53] and in the conclusion succeeds in informing the whole structure with the impression of dramatic unity. In throwing off the evil guidance of Mortimer and the Queen Mother, young King Edward III establishes a peace which becomes the point to which the previous action, infused with a purpose by the unified artistic conception, is then seen to tend. Marlowe's achievement consists of raising for the first time the chronicle-history genre to the level of tragedy.[54]

Shakespeare's *Richard III*, probably written only a year or two after *Edward II*, [55] reveals what Marlowe did not accomplish in the development of the tragic form. He could not conceive of an Earl of Richmond, untainted, heroic, defeating the wicked King Richard in single combat, and uniting forever the red rose with the white. Admittedly, the legends surrounding Richard's life and the famous battle of Bosworth Field lent themselves more readily than Marlowe's materials to the creation of a tragic hero and of a reconstructed order emergent from the hero's fall, but Marlowe's unfulfilled vision resulted at least as much from the pessimism of his temperament as from the unwieldiness of inherited forms and factual matter. Marlowe offers to show us a "toward" prince who compares himself with Atlas bearing the weight of the heavens (III, ii, 76–78); but we remember, rather, his father's metaphor: "he's a lamb, encompassèd by wolves" (V, i, 41).

The Tragicall History of the Life and Death of Doctor Faustus

Master of all his studies and "glutted now with learning's golden gifts" (Prologue, l. 24), Faustus nevertheless bemoans his constrained lot: "Yet art thou still but Faustus and a man" (I, i, 23). One hears in these words the essence of the discontent that drives each of Marlowe's heroes to disdain the shepherd's weeds of his common mortality and to soar toward a kind of divinity. Like Tamburlaine, Faustus would be a demigod on earth; like Barabas, he would rip up the bowels of the earth for fabulous treasures; and like Gaveston and Mortimer, he would command kings. Of humble birth, student (now doctor) of divinity, poet, playmaker, lover of beauty, he must have struck Marlowe when the playwright came upon him in the *English Faust Book*[56] as at once very much like himself and very like the grandest heroes of his drama.

The Renaissance neo-Platonist Pico della Mirandola, driven by a different kind of ambition, a "holy ambition,"[57] prescribed a path for a man to exceed the commonplace: through justice we attain the Throne; through intelligence we become Cherubim; and through love of God we are His Seraphim and at one with Him. For his part, however, Faustus dismisses, along with medicine, the disciplines of law ("justice"), philosophy ("intelligence"), and theology ("love of God") and delves into the illicit study of necromancy and conjuration. He completes Marlowe's own triad: with *virtù* one may overrule the world; with policy one may subvert it; and with black magic one may "be as Jove is in the sky, / Lord and commander of these elements" (I, i, 77–78).

Pico remains the indefatigable optimist, but Marlowe has turned from the exultation of *1 Tamburlaine* to the deep gloom of the ending of *Dr. Faustus:* the analogue for Faustus' quest is not the highest order of angels but the fallen order of which Lucifer and Mephistopheles are Prince and Arch-Regent; and in the end Faustus attains not oneness with God but banishment from Him. Death by disease ends Tamburlaine's life, human treachery traps Barabas in his own device, and Edward is deposed in the name of the people by a Machiavel; but in *Dr. Faustus* all the forces of darkness, all the superhuman manifestations of evil array themselves against man's salvation.

F. L. Lucas has written that "in tragedy is embodied the eternal contradiction between man's weakness and his courage, his stupidity and his magnificence, his frailty and his strength."[58] For tragedy to raise itself above homily, however, the playwright must upset the balance in favor of man's heroic grandeur: a fool destroyed by the human or superhuman forces that conspire his overthrow becomes a moral exemplum; a man of indomitable spirit "destroyed but not defeated" by an inimical universe is the material for a tragic hero. In *Dr. Faustus* the balance seems to weigh uncertainly: despite the grand defiance of the man who would teach the devil himself "manly fortitude" (I, iii, 85), there remains an underlying suspicion that only a fool would deny the existence of a hell of which Mephistopheles stands before him as proof, that only a trifler would conjure devils to play petty tricks on a horse-courser or a garrulous knight. J. P. Brockbank states the problem of ambiguity more than he resolves it when he says of the two aspects of the play, the "Morality and Heroic Tragedy," that "each in its own way triumphs over the other."[59]

The ambiguity of the play results, I would maintain, from the duality of Marlowe's own attitude towards Faustus' aspiration, his sense of both its glory and its folly. The celebration of the glory of hyperbolic aspiration has been remembered as Marlowe's signature; to Santayana, for example, Fautus suffered death in the noble pursuit of "everything that the Renaissance prized,—power, curious knowledge, enterprise, wealth, and beauty."[60] But the undercurrent of doubt and qualification, the intimations that Faustus' gigantic blasphemies and inflated "self-conceit" (Prologue, l. 20) have simply proved him blind to the "chiefest bliss" (Prologue, l. 27) of his soul, are likewise pervasive; and they are bodied forth in the character of the Old Man.

One may well dismiss the "cloistered virtue" of the three scholars and the pedestrian orthodoxy of the Good Angel as likely objects of Marlowe's scorn, but the Old Man's virtue is tested in the furnace of the devils' tortures and found true, his Christian faith is sifted with Satan's

pride and proved indestructible. In his fatherly sympathy
for Faustus and in his words of gentle admonition, Marlowe creates "a poetry of 'kind rebuke,' a moral music":[61]

> For, gentle son, I speak not in wrath
> Or envy of thee, but in tender love
> And pity of thy future misery.
>
> (V, i, 50–52)

When Faustus sounds the depths of his despair and would
kill himself with a dagger promptly provided by Mephistopheles, the Old Man stays his hand with the promise of
Christ's mercy: he sees a "vial full of precious grace"
(V, i, 62) ready to pour into Faustus' soul if he will re-
pent his sins. For the Old Man, as for Abigail, at the inner
temple of faith we find the "Son that gives eternal life"
(*The Jew,* III, iii, 65), the Savior whom Faustus earlier
denied by the omission of Christian mercy from his syllo-
gism dismissing the study of divinity (I, i, 38–49).

In the agony of his last hour, Faustus himself perceives
the means to his salvation:

See, see, where Christ's blood streams in the firmament!
One drop would save my soul, half a drop! Ah, my Christ!
(V, ii, 143–144)

He would leap up to his God but cannot, the vision passes,
and the revenging arm and wrathful brows of the Old

Testament God replace Christ's mercy. "Who pulls me down?" (V, ii, 142), Faustus demands, but the question remains unanswered. When pursued by the devils, the Old Man flees to the bosom of his God: his faith is pure and the doubt of this world poses no obstacles for him. But for Faustus, and ultimately, one feels, for Marlowe too, the haven of Christian grace hangs as remote as the firmament, and the terrible weight of knowledge and worldly experience pulls him down. In the context of Marlowe's entire canon of plays, Christ's grace stands not only for itself but for the agonist vision in general: for Zenocrate's pity and humble reverence, for Olympia's chaste honor, for Abigail's saddened piety, and for Prince Edward's innocence tempered with courage. Marlowe would reach out to these gentle virtues, would conceive of them as meaningful forces in a world of bitter hostilities, but in the end he falls back to the edge of the gaping hell-mouth.

Threatened by the presence of a moral grace which he can sense but not conceive for himself, Faustus would have Mephistopheles oppress the Old Man with the torments of "our hell" (V, i, 86). It is the moment of Faustus' deepest dive into evil—he reaffirms his allegiance to Lucifer with his own blood and commits the sin of demoniality (intercourse with a spirit) with Helen[62]—and it is, too, the moment of his highest soaring:

Here will I dwell, for heaven is in these lips,
And all is dross that is not Helena.

(V, i, 104–105)

The Old Man has no place in either realm of Faustus'
existence; he can only observe, lament, and then flee before
the onslaught of the devils. In his flight the schism
between the protagonist and the agonist has grown complete: no longer joined by marriage and mutual love as
in *Tamburlaine,* no longer even sharing the tenuous bonds
of kinship as in *Edward II* and *The Jew of Malta,* Faustus
and the Old Man are sundered by Faustus' animosity for
"that base and agèd man" (V, i, 84). In *Dr. Faustus* Marlowe denies the possibility of that harmony between ambition and salvation, between heroic *virtù* and Christian
virtue, which he once postulated in *1 Tamburlaine* but in
which he could no longer believe.[63]

More than simply undercutting the gigantic endeavors
of the protagonists, somewhat like dogs nipping at the
heels of giants, the agonists suggest—though only tenta-
tively, even when taken as a group—another way of
seeing and of living this life; and we must ask whether
this indeed is "the way leading out," out of the violence
and suffering and savage treacheries of *2 Tamburlaine, The
Jew of Malta,* and *Edward II,* out of the horror of damnation in *Dr. Faustus.* The agonists themselves achieve salvation in their virtuous lives and, some of them, in their

"good" deaths, but they fail to bring their goodness into the world. Theirs is a personal salvation only, and at the conclusions of the plays, except for Edward III's partial assertiveness they have abdicated to the chaos of defeated aspiration and triumphant mediocrity. The Old Man escapes unto his God, but he who sought to be more than a man and in the end begged to be less so that he might escape God's wrath discovers again the plight of man from which there is no way out:

Yet art thou still but Faustus and a man.

A NOTE ON A THEORY OF TRAGEDY

It would be fatuous to embark at this point a discussion of theories of tragedy, but it would likewise be neglectful not to draw one close-at-hand conclusion about one difference between Marlowe's and Shakespeare's tragic visions. An important distinction between the two tragedians derives from the foregoing treatment of Marlowe's plays. The general absence of strong, attractive, and virtuous characters at the ends of Marlowe's tragedies makes impossible the emergence of a revitalized vision of life in them, whether it be a new political, social, or spiritual order; and it consequently deepens the gloom of Marlowe's tragic vision to something without the underlying strength of affirmation that characterizes the great Shakespearean tragedies.

Among the many attempted resolutions of the paradox of tragedy—the strange fact of human psychology that in watching or reading about the misfortunes of a tragic hero we find pleasure or "metaphysical comfort"[64]—a number of them attribute at least part of this pleasure to our perception, through the eyes of the tragedian, of an indestructible strain of good immanent in the world order.

From this point of view, the tragic mood is born of a conflict between faith and doubt, good and evil, the Apollonian and the Dionysian;[65] and the viewer of tragedy is saved from despair by a redeeming vision of man's dignity and the world's beauty which survives the riot of suffering and evil.

Nietzsche, for instance, wrote: "the truly existent primal unity, eternally suffering and contradictory, also needs the rapturous vision, the pleasurable illusion, for its continuous redemption";[66] and to the Greek satyr chorus he ascribed the function of reestablishing the Apollonian faith in ordered beauty. Among twentieth-century critics, Una Ellis-Fermor, in her discussion of the "equilibrium of tragedy," wrote: "Beyond the realization of evil and pain . . . there is the perception, at once more comprehensive and less explicit, of a possible resolution, of some reconciliation with or interpretation in terms of good."[67] Their theories do not envision the idealized world of Hegelian tragedy where justice never fails and where all discords merge into a higher order of harmony,[68] but they recognize an undercurrent of rebirth which coexists in the richest tragedy with a profound awareness of the naked horror of existence.

The dualism of vision in Marlowe's tragedies is paralleled in Shakespeare by the omnipresent conflict of world views or, equally, of attitudes toward human nature:

43

What a piece of work is a man, how noble in
reason, how infinite in faculties . . . and
yet to me, what is this quintessence of dust?
(*Hamlet*, II, ii, 312ff)

What Marlowe could not achieve, however, what he
seemed to long to conceive but never succeeded in
bringing to fruition except partially in *Edward II* is that
which Ellis-Fermor describes in Shakespeare, as well as
Aeschylus, Sophocles, and Ibsen: "though the evidence
of pain and evil is never denied, the final position is not
despair or rebellion, but a perception of that in man's
destiny which resolves pain in exultation."[69] One finds no
exultation at the end of *Dr. Faustus*: with the torture and
flight of the good Old Man and with only the plodding
conventionality of the scholars and chorus left to ser-
monize upon Faustus' death, the conclusion is filled solely
with the unseeing despair and violent rebellion of Faustus' last minutes. In *King Lear* Shakespeare presents suf-
ferings of like terror, but from the moment of Lear's kind
gesture towards his Fool (III, ii, 68–69), a newly awaken-
ing sensitivity in Lear himself gives hope for man's capacity for growth and renewal. And the survival of Edgar,
Kent, and Albany, their valor and grace (in a non-Christian
sense) proved by trial, gives promise of a renewed effort
to make a better world.

As Lear's personal rebirth in the midst of his downfall

suggests, the sense of triumph over despair can be communicated by various means of form and content.[70] I note here simply that the surviving presence of appealing characters who relate both to the tragic hero and to the audience contributes significantly in Shakespeare and other tragedians to the full and satisfying meaning of tragedy, and that the absence of such characters, besides contributing to the moral ambiguity of his plays, makes Marlowe's tragedies more fiercely pessimistic and less spiritually fulfilling than Shakespeare's tragic masterpieces.

BIBLIOGRAPHY

NOTES

BIBLIOGRAPHY

I. Plays

The Famous Victories of Henry the Fifth. In *Chief Pre-Shake-spearean Dramas,* ed. Joseph Quincy Adams. Cambridge, Mass., 1924.

The Farce of the Worthy Master Pierre Patelin, trans. M. A. Jagendorf. In *World Drama,* ed. Barrett H. Clark. 2 vols. London, 1933.

Greene, Robert. *The Plays and Poems of Robert Greene,* ed. J. Churton Collins. 2 vols. Oxford, 1905.

Kyd, Thomas. *The Works of Thomas Kyd,* ed. Frederick S. Boas. Oxford, 1901.

Marlowe, Christopher. *The Complete Plays of Christopher Marlowe,* ed. Irving Ribner. New York, 1963.

———— *Edward II,* ed. H. B. Charlton and T. D. Waller. Methuen Series. New York, 1966.

———— *The Jew of Malta and The Massacre at Paris,* ed. H. S. Bennett. Methuen Series. New York, 1966.

———— *Marlowe's Poems,* ed. L. C. Martin. Methuen Series. New York, 1966.

———— *Tamburlaine the Great,* ed. Una M. Ellis-Fermor. Methuen Series. New York, 1966.

Peele, George. *The Works of Peele,* ed. A. H. Bullen. 2 vols. London, 1888.

Preston, Thomas. *The Life of Cambises, King of Percia.* In *Chief Pre-Shakespearean Dramas,* ed. Joseph Quincy Adams. Cambridge, Mass., 1924.

Shakespeare, William. *The Signet Classic Shakespeare,* ed. Sylvan Barnet. New York, 1963.

W[ilson], R[obert]. *The Three Ladies of London,* ed. John S. Farmer. Tudor Facsimile Texts. N.p., 1911.

Woodes, Robert. *The Conflict of Conscience.* In vol. VI of *Old English Plays,* ed. Robert Dodsley, rev. by W. Carew Hazlitt. 15 vols. London, 1874.

—— *The Conflict of Conscience.* Malone Society Reprints. Oxford, 1952.

II. Critical Studies of Marlowe, and Related Works

Bevington, David M. *From "Mankind" to Marlowe: Growth of Structure in the Popular Drama of Tudor England.* Cambridge, Mass., 1962.

Bowers, Fredson Thayer. *Elizabethan Revenge Tragedy, 1587–1642.* Princeton, 1940.

Briggs, William Dinsmore, ed. *Marlowe's "Edward II."* London, 1914.

Brooke, C. F. Tucker, ed. *The Life of Marlowe and "The Tragedy of Dido, Queen of Carthage."* Methuen Series. New York, 1966.

Chambers, E. K. *The Elizabethan Stage.* 4 vols. Oxford, 1936.

Cole, Douglas. *Suffering and Evil in the Plays of Christopher Marlowe.* Princeton, 1962.

Craig, Hardin. *The Enchanted Glass: The Elizabethan Mind in Literature.* New York, 1936.

Eliot, T. S. "Notes on the Blank Verse of Christopher Marlowe." In *The Sacred Wood: Essays on Poetry and Criticism.* London, 1928.

—— "Shakespeare and the Stoicism of Seneca." In *Selected Essays, 1917–1932.* New York, 1932.

Empson, William. "Two Proper Crimes," *The Nation,* CLXIII (October 1946), 444–445.

Farnham, Willard. *The Medieval Heritage of Elizabethan Tragedy.* Berkeley, 1936.

Gardner, Helen L. "The Second Part of *Tamburlaine the Great," Modern Language Review,* XXXVII (January 1942), 18–24.

Harbage, Alfred. *Annals of English Drama, 975 1700,* rev. by Samuel Schoenbaum. London, 1964.

———— *Shakespeare's Audience.* New York, 1941.

Hillier, Richard L. "The Imagery of Color, Light and Darkness in the Poetry of Christopher Marlowe," *University of Colorado Studies,* ser. B, II (October 1945), 101–125.

Holinshed, Raphaell. *The Laste Volume of the Chronicles of England, Scotlande, and Irelande.* 2 vols. London, 1577.

Jump, John D., ed. *Dr. Faustus.* The Revels Plays. Cambridge, Mass., 1965.

Kocher, Paul H. *Christopher Marlowe: His Thought, Learning and Character.* New York, 1962.

Leech, Clifford, ed. *Marlowe: A Collection of Critical Essays.* Twentieth Century Views Series. Englewood Cliffs, 1964.

Levin, Harry. "Marlowe Today," *Tulane Drama Review,* VIII (Summer 1964), 25–31.

———— *The Overreacher: A Study of Christopher Marlowe.* Cambridge, Mass., 1952.

Pico della Mirandola, Giovanni. "Oration on the Dignity of Man." In *Renaissance Philosophy,* ed. and trans. Arturo B. Fallico and Herman Shapiro. 2 vols. New York, 1967.

Rose, William, ed. *The Historie of the Damnable Life, and Deserved Death of Doctor John Faustus.* Notre Dame, 1963.

Sanders, Wilbur. *The Dramatist and the Received Idea:*

Studies in the Plays of Marlowe and Shakespeare. Cambridge, Eng., 1968.

Santayana, George. *Three Philosophical Poets: Lucretius, Dante, and Goethe.* Cambridge, Mass., 1927.

Sidney, Sir Philip. "An Apologie for Poetrie." In *Elizabethan Critical Essays,* ed. G. Gregory Smith. 2 vols. Oxford, 1904.

Smith, Hallett. "Tamburlaine and the Renaissance," *University of Colorado Studies,* ser. B, II (October 1945), 126–131.

Tillyard, E. M. W. *Shakespeare's History Plays.* New York, 1962.

Waith, Eugene M. *"Edward II:* The Shadow of Action," *Tulane Drama Review,* VIII (Summer 1964), 59–76.

———— *The Herculean Hero in Marlowe, Chapman, Shakespeare and Dryden.* New York, 1962.

Wilson, F. P. *Marlowe and the Early Shakespeare.* Oxford, 1953.

III. Theories of Tragedy

Butcher, S. H. *Aristotle's Theory of Poetry and Fine Art.* London, 1907.

Ellis-Fermor, Una M. *The Frontiers of Drama.* London, 1946.

Lucas, F. L. *Tragedy in Relation to Aristotle's "Poetics."* London, 1930.

Nietzsche, Friedrich. *The Birth of Tragedy and The Case of Wagner,* trans. Walter Kaufmann. New York, 1967.

Raphael, D. D. *The Paradox of Tragedy.* London, 1960.

Richards, I. A. *Principles of Literary Criticism.* London, 1960.

Weisinger, Herbert. *Tragedy and the Paradox of the Fortunate Fall.* London, 1953.

NOTES

1. My discussion of the morality play tradition is indebted to David M. Bevington, *From "Mankind" to Marlowe: Growth of Structure in the Popular Drama of Tudor England* (Cambridge, Mass., 1962).

2. Lecture by Alfred Harbage, English 125a, "Tudor Drama to Jonson," Harvard University, 1969–70.

3. In speaking of Marlowe's plays I will consider only *1* and *2 Tamburlaine, The Jew of Malta, Edward II*, and *Dr. Faustus*. Besides being of lesser quality, *The Tragedy of Dido, Queen of Carthage* was not written for the popular theater, and *The Massacre at Paris* survives only in a badly mutilated text (see Bevington, p. 199). Citations from Marlowe are to *The Complete Plays*, ed. Irving Ribner (New York, 1963). Following Ribner and others, I will treat the five plays to be discussed as if composed in the order listed above.

4. These figures are taken from William Wager's *Enough is as Good as a Feast* (1560), Ulpian Fulwell's *Like Will to Like, Quoth the Devil to the Collier* (1568), and the anonymous *Trial of Treasure* (1567), respectively. The dating of all plays in this discussion, unless otherwise noted, is in accordance with that of Alfred Harbage in *Annals of English Drama, 975–1700*, rev. by Samuel Schoenbaum (London, 1964). Dates correspond to the most probable year of the first performance rather than to the first printing.

5. See Wilbur Sanders, *The Dramatist and the Received Idea: Studies in the Plays of Marlowe and Shakespeare* (Cambridge, Eng., 1968), p. 55.

6. William Shakespeare, *Troilus and Cressida,* ed. Daniel

Seltzer, Signet Classic Shakespeare Series, ed. Sylvan Barnet (New York, 1963), I, iii, 86. All line references from Shakespeare in this discussion will be quoted from the Signet Classic Series.

7. As in William Wager's *The Longer Thou Livest the More Fool Thou Art* (1559). See Bevington, p. 162.

8. Written by a group of authors and first printed in 1599 by John Wayland, the *Mirror for Magistrates* was conceived as an extension of John Lydgate's translation and redaction of Boccaccio's *De casibus virorum illustrium* (1363–1364), called *Fall of Princes* (ca. 1440); it was instrumental in reviving the *de casibus* tradition of tragedy on the Elizabethan stage. See Willard Farnham, *The Medieval Heritage of Elizabethan Tragedy* (Berkeley, 1936), pp. 271–303.

9. "Preface," *Perimedes* (1588), quoted in C. F. Tucker Brooke, ed., *The Life of Marlowe and "The Tragedy of Dido, Queen of Carthage," The Works and Life of Christopher Marlowe,* ed. R. H. Case, Methuen Series (London, 1966)—hereafter cited as *Works*—p. 44.

10. See Harry Levin, *The Overreacher: A Study of Christopher Marlowe* (Cambridge, Mass., 1952), pp. 1–27.

11. Thomas Beard, "Of Epicures and Atheists," *The Theatre of Gods Iudgements* (1597), quoted in Brooke, ed., *The Life and "Dido,"* p. 112.

12. See Harry Levin, "Marlowe Today," *Tulane Drama Review,* VIII (Summer 1964), 25–31.

13. Paul H. Kocher, *Christopher Marlowe: His Thought, Learning and Character* (New York, 1962), p. 4.

14. Levin, "Marlowe Today," p. 28.

15. See E. K. Chambers, *The Elizabethan Stage* (Oxford, 1923), I, 318.

16. P. 261.

17. The linear sequence, as described by Bevington, is one from innocence to plotting to downfall to retribution and possibly to recovery; see pp. 142, 144, 166.

18. *Dido,* IV, iii, 12 and II, i, 186, quoted by Levin, *The Overreacher,* p. 22.

19. For a brief discussion of the role of boy actors in the popular theater, see Bevington, pp. 74–79, 105–106, 125–127.

20. The Baines Note makes this allegation; see Brooke, ed., *The Life and "Dido,"* p. 63.

21. Michael Drayton, "To Henry Reynolds, of Poets and Poesie," *The Battaile of Agincourt, Elegies, etc.* (1627), p. 206, quoted in Brooke, ed., *The Life and "Dido,"* p. 80.

22. Bishop Hall, *Vergidemiae* (1597), quoted in Brooke, ed., *The Life and "Dido,"* p. 49, n. 1.

23. Levin, *The Overreacher,* pp. 11–15.

24. Eugene M. Waith, *The Herculean Hero in Marlowe, Chapman, Shakespeare and Dryden* (New York, 1962), pp. 69–70.

25. This point is made by Bevington, p. 213, and by F. P. Wilson, *Marlowe and the Early Shakespeare* (Oxford, 1953), p. 19.

26. Evidence to this effect includes the fact that Marlowe used virtually all the biographical material from his sources in Part One (see Una M. Ellis-Fermor, ed., *Tamburlaine the Great,* in *Works,* p. 41) and the first three lines of the Prologue to *2 Tamburlaine:* "The general welcomes Tamburlaine received, / When he arrivèd last upon our stage, / Hath made our poet pen his Second Part."

27. Sir Philip Sidney, "An Apologie for Poetrie" (1595), in *Elizabethan Critical Essays,* ed. G. Gregory Smith (Oxford, 1904), I, 177.

28. I have used here the date given by J. Churton Collins

in his edition of *The Plays and Poems of Robert Greene* (Oxford, 1905), I, 74–75, on the strength of the evidence which he cites.

29. *The Battle of Alcazar* (1589), I, ii, 34, in *The Works of George Peele*, ed. A. H. Bullen (London, 1888), I, 237.

30. Waith stresses cruelty as one of the characteristic qualities of the Herculean hero; see *The Herculean Hero*, p. 75.

31. See, for instance, Levin, *The Overreacher*, pp. 30–54; Ellis-Fermor, ed., *Tamburlaine the Great*, pp. 50, 53–55; and Helen L. Gardner, "The Second Part of *Tamburlaine the Great*," *Modern Language Review*, XXXVII (January 1942), 18–24.

32. See *2 Tamburlaine*, Prologue, ll. 1–3. Harbage gives the data of Henslowe's receipts at the Rose Theater between June 1594 and July 1597, indicating the popularity of *1 Tamburlaine* when performed in revival: see *Shakespeare's Audience* (New York, 1941), p. 178.

33. Ellis-Fermor also discusses the relation between the form of the play and Marlowe's changed attitude; see *Tamburlaine the Great*, pp. 48–61.

34. See Ellis-Fermor, ed., *Tamburlaine the Great*, p. 7, n. 2, where she cites six or seven specific passages from each of the two parts to demonstrate "the darker audacity" of Part Two. All the passages cited from the second part follow Zenocrate's death.

35. See Bevington, p. 208.

36. See Gardner, p. 22.

37. See Ellis-Fermor, ed., *Tamburlaine the Great*, p. 44.

38. See Ellis-Fermor, ed., *Tamburlaine the Great*, pp. 17–48.

39. Tudor Facsimile Texts, ed. John S. Farmer (n.p., 1911), sig. F.

40. Trans. M. A. Jagendorf, in *World Drama*, ed. Barrett H.

Clark (London, 1933), I, 337–360. The date cited for this French play is taken from this volume.

41. "Notes on the Blank Verse of Christopher Marlowe," in *The Sacred Wood: Essays on Poetry and Criticism* (London, 1928), p. 92.

42. See Fredson Thayer Bowers, *Elizabethan Revenge Tragedy, 1587–1642* (Princeton, 1940), pp. 104–109.

43. As other examples of this double exposure technique, note Barabas' mock despair in conversation with the other Jews (I, ii, 171ff) followed by his real despair when he learns that he will not be allowed to enter his house, now a convent, to recover his hidden money (I, ii, 258ff); and note his counterfeit death followed by his real death.

44. See, for instance, Abigail's dying request to Friar Barnardine: "Convert my father that he may be saved" (III, vi, 38), and the words of her counterpart, Jessica, in Shakespeare's *Merchant of Venice:* "I shall be saved by my husband. He hath made me a Christian" (III, v, 18–19).

45. Levin, p. 70.

46. See Sanders, pp. 52–53; and Levin, *The Overreacher,* pp. 76–77.

47. Raphaell Holinshed, *The Laste [Second] Volume of the Chronicles of England, Scotlande, and Irelande* (London, 1577), p. 883. These words are also quoted in H. B. Charlton and R. D. Waller, eds., *Edward II,* in *Works,* pp. 203–204, note to V, v, 113.

48. See E. M. W. Tillyard, *Shakespeare's History Plays,* (New York, 1962), 78–85.

49. *Marlowe and the Early Shakespeare,* p. 94.

50. *Richard II,* II, i, 31.

51. My knowledge of chronicle histories prior to Marlowe and Shakespeare derives chiefly from William Dinsmore

Briggs, ed., *Marlowe's "Edward II"* (London, 1914), pp. ix–cxxx.

52. See Briggs, ed., *Marlowe's "Edward II,"* p. cix.

53. See Levin, *The Overreacher,* p. 189.

54. Briggs, ed., *Marlowe's "Edward II,"* p. cix.

55. Harbage dates *Edward II* in 1592 and *Richard III* in 1593; see *Annals of English Drama,* pp. 56, 58.

56. William Rose, ed., *The Historie of the Damnable Life, and Deserved Death of Doctor John Faustus* (1592) (Notre Dame, 1963).

57. Giovanni Pico della Mirandola, "Oration on the Dignity of Man," in *Renaissance Philosophy,* ed. and trans. Arturo B. Fallico and Herman Shapiro (New York, 1967), I, 146.

58. *Tragedy in Relation to Aristotle's "Poetics"* (London, 1930), p. 55.

59. "The Damnation of Faustus," in *Marlowe: A Collection of Critical Essays,* ed. Clifford Leech (Englewood Cliffs, 1964), p. 116.

60. George Santayana, *Three Philosophical Poets: Lucretius, Dante, and Goethe* (Cambridge, Mass., 1927), p. 149.

61. J. P. Brockbank, "The Damnation of Faustus," p. 112.

62. See W. W. Greg, "The Damnation of Faustus," in *Marlowe: A Collection of Critical Essays,* ed. Clifford Leech (Englewood Cliffs, 1964), pp. 104–107.

63. Although one is tempted to discern a progressive, play-to-play deepening of Marlowe's pessimistic spirit from *1 Tamburlaine* to *Dr. Faustus,* uncertainty as to the order of composition of the plays makes this observation unfounded, though perhaps not incorrect. If, for instance, Edward III was the last agonist created by Marlowe, one might find a slight narrowing of the schism between agonist and protagonist in Marlowe's final work. Nevertheless, the contrast in moods between

1 Tamburlaine and *Edward II* is as great as between *1 Tamburlaine* and *Dr. Faustus;* as Eugene Waith has written, "Where *Tamburlaine* seems to open up ever wider prospects . . . *Edward II* closes down until the focus is upon a prison, a deathbed, a bier" (*"Edward II:* The Shadow of Action," *Tulane Drama Review,* VIII [Summer 1964], 76). The important conclusion to be drawn as to Marlowe's development as a playwright, however, is not in terms of gradations of pessimism or degrees of antagonism between characters; it is that a split, not present in *1 Tamburlaine* and only beginning to appear in *2 Tamburlaine,* does develop between the protagonists and the agonists of the three later plays. This split is an expression of Marlowe's ambivalence towards his giant heroes and of the irreconcilability between two sides of his character that helped to spawn the fierce pessimism of his tragic vision.

64. Friedrich Nietzsche, *The Birth of Tragedy and The Case of Wagner,* trans. Walter Kaufmann (New York, 1967), p. 59.

65. The terminology, of course, is from Nietzsche's description of the two visions of life and art feeding into Greek tragedy. Other critics not mentioned in the text who perceive this "Manichean" conflict in tragedy include I. A. Richards (*Principles of Literary Criticism* [London, 1960], pp. 245–248); Lucas (*Tragedy,* pp. 9–58); and Herbert Weisinger (*Tragedy and the Paradox of the Fortunate Fall* [London, 1953], pp. 7–111, 228–273).

66. *The Birth of Tragedy,* p. 45.

67. *The Frontiers of Drama* (London, 1946), p. 128.

68. My understanding of Hegel's theory of tragedy is taken from Lucas' treatment of it; see *Tragedy,* pp. 40–43.

69. *The Frontiers of Drama,* p. 130.

70. The distinction between form and content, while always an artificial dichotomy in art, is made here to distinguish

factors like the perfection of language or the integrity in presentation of life (see Lucas, pp. 57–58) from the function, related both to content and form, of the virtuous characters who survive to the conclusion.